VOICES

FROM THE CLOUD

(WORDS WELL WORTH WRITING)

BY

DR. JEAN NORBERT AUGUSTIN

Table of Contents

To the Father, the Son and the Holy Spirit without whose inspiration this Anthology would not have been written.

"And the Lord said unto Moses, Lol, I come unto thee in a thick cloud, that people may hear when I speak with thee, and believe thee for ever. And Moses told the words of the people unto the Lord" (Exodus 19:9, KJV).

"While he yet spoke, behold, a bright cloud overshadowed them: and behold a voice out of the cloud, which said, This is my beloved Son, in whom I am well pleased; hear ye him," (Matthew 17:5, KJV).

Preface

My first contact with English poetry was when I became a High School student in 1960. We had to study a book aptly titled "The Journey Begins". However, the journey was not very smooth during my first three years. Teachers would come and go. Consequently, the foundation was not properly laid.

Things started to become serious and interesting when I was in fourth year. We had good teachers and we were introduced to odes and sonnets. We discovered rhymes, meters, iambic feet, alliterations, personifications and so on.

In my fifth year, a book was prescribed, titled "Anthology of Longer Poems". Then started and was developed my real love for poetry. I particularly enjoyed reading Keats, Wordsworth, Byron, Milton, Southey, Shirley, Cowper and so many others.

As I studied Shakespearean plays, I discovered the beauty and richness of seventeenth century English. Many of my classmates found it difficult to cope with it. But, for me, the vocabulary and the phraseology of the plays were a real pleasure.

That's why I enjoy reading the King James Bible while many prefer the more modern and simpler versions.

Back in the nineties, an idea occurred to me: why not try to rewrite one or two Bible episodes in verse form? I sat down and started writing, trying to find proper rhymes while giving sense to the narratives and respecting Biblical conformity.

After a few satisfactory attempts, I somehow left off and forgot the poems.

Until I rediscovered them in the hard disk of my computer. Others were scribbled and lay hidden in an old diary.

Then Jesus' teaching on the Parable of the Talents came to my mind. Unearthing my talents, I set out to make them fructify.

The more I wrote, the easier the exercise became. Sometimes, at night, a Bible episode would come to my mind and I would struggle with it to mentally give it shape. The difficult part was to mentally repeat my nocturnal findings over and over until morning came when I could note down my thoughts and ideas lest I forget.

In this Anthology, not only are there Biblical narratives, but -what I like best – there are those reflective, introspective poems which I find quite original.

I have also included a few psalms written in free verse.

Such an accomplishment has to be nothing less than the work of the Holy Spirit within me. The inspiration came – nay, flowed so easily and so incessantly that it had to come from the river of divine inspiration and not emanate from human intellect.

I give glory to God's Holy Spirit for this work and trust it will be instrumental in helping you rediscover the beauty of the Holy Scriptures and bring at least some to salvation through faith in Jesus Christ.

Dr. Jean Norbert Augustin.

Acknowledgements

My wholehearted thanks go to

My son Sheldon for his precious advice and help

My daughter-in-law Priscilla for assistance with

the initial layout,

My wife Maryse and my daughter Sharon for their

constant support.

I.

THE CREATION
(Genesis 1)

Heavens, I command ye to be!
And, in the vast above, fix ye!
Earth, at My Word, come down
And, to the world, be thou the ground!
Sun, set thee above to mark the day
And thee, moon, at night shine in the milky way!
Stars and galaxies, the azure adorn
Till the sun outshines ye at dawn!
Below, I command trees to grow
And brooks and rivers to flow!
May there be birds in the air,
Fishes in the sea and cattle everywhere!
Now, let's make of all the very best –
The magnitude of our love to manifest:
Man let us make now in our own likeness
To show above all of creation his highness.
Over all creation, let's make him king
So he can rule over the fish, the fowl and every living
thing.
Down there he'll manifest our glory
And, like us up here live for all eternity.

2.

MAYHEM IN EDEN
(Genesis 3)

When Adam and Eve sinned in Eden,
Harmony in the Garden was broken.
By the Serpent of old bitten,
Man to Heaven became alien.

Despising the Tree of Life,
Guilty husband and wife
Eating of the Tree of Good and Evil,
They chose to do the Devil's will.

Thinking their sin to hide,
In bushes went they to hide
In the Almighty's Presence not to abide.
With leaves to dress they tried.

But how long their leafy garb would stand
Under the sun of such a torrid land?
Almighty God, in His mercy,
Their nakedness at once did see.

Of two animals the blood He shed
With skins Adam and Eve to clothe instead.
But how mankind could God redeem –
A most difficult thing it all did seem!

Then stood Jesus, saying: "Father, be still,
Lo, I come today to do Thy will!"
Indeed, in human garb He dressed
So, once redressed, mankind could then be blessed.

(Written on 22 July at 1:00)

3.

THE PLAN CONCEIVED

One gloomy day in Eternity past,
The Father wept when things went wrong:
Man into Hell, the Devil had resolved to cast!
But, merciful, the Father wouldn't let this last long.
Turning to Jesus on His majestic Throne,
The Father said: "Man has fallen into sin
And now he finds himself all alone,
Lamenting over the mess he's put himself in."
"But, for him, such love have I, Son,
That I'll save him from eternal damnation!
The problem is that I can see none
Worthy to die and secure man's redemption."
"Why worry, Father," came Jesus's reply.
"Am I not worthy man's sins to atone?
Is my Blood not potent enough to cry
For mercy upon humanity dethroned?"
"Nay, My Son, Thy Blood is mighty
And potent and powerful enough every sin to blot.
But Thou wilt have to clothe humanity ..."
"Why worry?" said the Spirit, "I sure can help, can I
not?"

4.
THE PROMISE MADE TO ABRAM
(Genesis 12 – 17)

I

Neath the Mesopotamian sky,
Where the impious Chaldeans lived,
Sat Abram and his wife Sarai,
From their hard daily chores relieved —
Their fat woolly flocks fleeced and fed,
Their meal taken, their fire dead.

II

As they sat musing, Abram said:
"See, Sarai, our sight daily fades,
Soon in the grave we shall be laid
To spend Eternity in Hades
Grey hair have we, but not an heir —
Save our man-servant, Eliezer!

III

Replied Sarai with muffled voice:
"The Lord since long my womb has locked
Lest o'er a son's birth I rejoice.
And now by all I'm daily mocked.
Having been cursed with barrenness,

My sole dowry to you is sadness!"

IV

As the poor couple sat and sobbed,
There came a Voice as from nowhere,
Such that, of their peace, they were robbed.
"Good news with you come I to share;
Come outside and the tidings hear!"
Resounded the Voice, loud and clear.

V

Out went the pair with anxiety,
To know what those tidings could be.
Walking like cats on hot ambers,
Sarai — though the blessing was hers —
Could not the situation grasp,
Her days of faith having elapsed!

VI

Nobody, nothing did Abram first see.
Then there occurred something extraordinary:
By faith, he could fully sense:
Of Someone the awesome Presence
Again the loud Voice spoke: "Abram!"
"Lord!" the old man said, "Here I am!"

VII

"Lift your head, look at the Heavens.
Seest thou all the stars above?

6

Now try to count them, if thou canst.
My own Hands made them out of love
So the night sky wouldn't be dull
And they could Man to slumber lull."

VIII

Shaking his head, Abram replied:
"Who can the heavenly hosts count?
Their myriads cannot be denied,
Nor of their beauty the amount!
Indeed, their majestic splendour
Is to Man a nightly wonder!"

IX

"You've been grieved for want of an heir
And you have been anxious to know
Whether it's not to Eliezer
Your wealth, after you're gone, will go...
But before your wife's called to the tomb,
A son she'll bear out of her womb!"

X

Laughter unable to repress,
Sarai said: "Oh, please, don't mock me.
How can such a crippled mistress
Like me, still bring forth a baby?
The fire of love has long been dead
And in no wise can now be fed."

7

XI

"Why didst thou laugh?" the Voice chided.
"Dost thou think I can't realize
What solemnly I've decided?
In time it shall materialize —
Know that I am the Great I AM,
And My Word always stands, Abram!"

XII

Then the awesome Presence lifted
And the Voice was heard no longer.
Happy to have thus been gifted,
The couple went in to ponder
Over that night's strange happenings:
"Tonight," said they, "we have witnessed strange
things!"

XIII

It was like wings their faith had grown!
Those words in their hearts they cherished.
But soon Sarai started to moan
And her faith sadly diminished.
On God's Word she no longer stood
And thought that bring some help she should!

XIV

She had a slave woman called Hagar.
One sad day arrived, all the same,
When she told Abram: "Go to her

And beget a son in my name.
That must be what the Lord implied,
Or else, how can I have that child?"

XV

And so to Hagar, Abram went.
But soon, his mistake its fruit bore!
For, when Hagar became pregnant,
Her mistress she obeyed no more!
She despised her and abased her,
Knowing she had Abram's favour.

XVI

But Sarai went to her husband
To stigmatize the attitude
Of the Egyptian slave woman.
Learning how Hagar had been rude,
Abram granted his wife's request
That she be rid of such a pest.

XVII

Having out of the house been chased,
Into the wild Hagar wandered.
Being with child, she soon tired
And was with thirst and hunger faced.
By chance, she spied a cool fountain
And lay down there to ease her pain.

XVIII

Reflecting upon her sad plight
And awaiting solace in death,
She suddenly saw a bright light
That caused her to run out of breath.
There stood an Angel of the Lord —
To rejoice she could now afford!

XIX

"Hagar, I've seen your affliction.
However, because you're with child,
Go back in complete submission
To the mistress you have defiled.
Ishmael you'll call your son's name,
To him I'll give repute and fame.

XX

He'll give birth to many nations
But a wild life he'll have to live
Full of perils and commotions.
My blessing, though, he'll receive."
Comforted by what she'd been told,
The stray sheep went back to her fold.

XXI

Again unto Abram God spake,
Recalling unto him His Word:
"With thee a great covenant I make
Such as no-one has ever heard!
A son thou shalt have for a fact
And thou shalt call him Isaac.

10

XXII

That son of Sarai shall be born.
Her sad heart shall henceforth rejoice
And no more shall she be forlorn.
She'll now sing with melodious voice.
Her prolonged curse shall be removed
And of men she'll now be approved.

XXIII

Her son shall be great among men
And shall be father to nations.
The land shall he fill with children.
If, Abram, thou hast some patience,
My Word thou shalt see accomplished
Exactly the way I have wished."

XXIV

But old Abram was skeptical:
"How can a hundred- year- old man —
It would seem most impractical —
And a ninety- year- old woman
A son at such ages beget?
May these blessings Ishmael get!"

XXV

"Nay, Ishmael shall bear a seed
That shall surely most fruitful be.
But I with Isaac, indeed,
Shall, by My own Divine Decree,

11

My precious covenant establish,
Which, in due time, I'll accomplish.

XXVI

Thy name henceforth shan't be Abram
Nor shall thy wife's name be Sarai.
Thy name I change to Abraham
To prove we're bound by a new tie.
And Sarah shall thy wife be called.
Hold firm to what you have been told!"

XXVII

With time, Sarah a son did bear
And called him Isaac, indeed.
The child enjoyed his parents' care
And grew up under their strict lead.
But soon hostility arose
That Abraham's two sons opposed!

XXVIII

Being of the two the elder,
Ishmael Isaac did tease.
The lad treated his young brother
Such that Sarah was sore displeased:
The mother and her wayward child
She ordered off into the wild!

XXIX

Abraham's heart broke with despair

Because of Ishmael, his son.
But, for his family's welfare,
Troublemaker he would spare none!
So he packed up some drink and food
And the pair sent he away for good!

XXX

In Hagar's and Sarah's story,
The Holy Bible teaches us
Lies a mighty allegory.
And that is what we'll now discuss.
These two women, they represent
Alliances quite different.

XXXI

Hagar and Ishmael an alliance
They represent that's temporal.
With them Sarah is at variance
For hers is rather spiritual:
One represents what is earthly,
And the other what's heavenly.

XXXII

Born of a foreign slave woman,
By pure human activity,
Ishmael represents such men
As are still in captivity.
It's of the Law a clear image —
Perfect picture of sheer bondage!

Born out of legitimacy,
By God's sole Sovereign volition,
Isaac, instead, stands for he
Who in Jesus seeks Redemption.
It is a clear image of Grace —
Divine Love for the human race!

5.

THE NATIVITY
(Luke 2; Matthew 2)

Here I am, in this poor manger laid
By Joseph, the carpenter, and Mary, the virgin maid.
Woolly bleating sheep around me gather from the
fold,
Out of mercy, to keep me from the cold,
Recognizing the new-born Lamb from above,
Sent down by their Maker as a gift of love.

Not a place in the inns for me was found
And yet, for love alone have I come down!
How inhospitable and cold this world has grown!
It's no longer the peaceful place I'd known!
Was it not perfect when my Father and I created it?
Yet, to receive me, there's but this place most unfit!

How different it is up there in my Father's presence
Where holy seraphim's and cherubim's pay us
obeisance!
But, coming down to this world was of my own volition
For the sole purpose of purchasing Man's
redemption.
Yet, they will betray me, curse me and spit into my
face.

But I, to do my Father's will, have come to offer grace.

On a Cross, a thorny crown will they put upon my head,
With nails and a spear will they bleed me till I'm dead.
But how futile and silly of them trying to put to death
The One who gives life and has power over their breath!
In the distance, over the hills, I can hear angels trumpeting
"Hallelujah! Today, in Bethlehem, is born unto ye a new King!

From the East, Magi - wise men of high eminence –
Are coming to pay me homage with gold, myrrh and incense.
But Herod Antipas – the Devil's hit-man –
In his folly, has ordered the deaths of innocent children
In an attempt me – the Lord, Saviour and Messiah – to kill,
Thereby accomplishing the Serpent of old's evil will.

In a while, poor Mary, Joseph and me, on a donkey,
Down to safer Egypt will have to flee.
But, do what they will, the Father's will
Will they never be able to bring to nil!
To the Cross on Golgotha Hill, will I inexorably go to die –
My holy blood to shed and sinful humanity to justify!

6.

THE PREACHING OF JOHN THE BAPTIST
(Luke 3: 1 – 18)

When John began his ministry,
Down to the Jordan went he
To call people to repentance
Before the day of the Lord's vengeance.

Scribes and Pharisees
Soldiers and Sadducees
People from every class and caste
Came to cast away their sins -present and past!

"You, brood of vipers," rebuked he,
"Who told you the Lord's anger to flee?"
Already the axe is put to the tree
His winnowing fan brings He!"

When asked to give your coat,
Do not refuse to give also your cloak.
When asked to go one mile,
Go two if you are not senile!

Soldiers, make no abuse of authority
Show no iniquity, but work with equity!
Doctors of the Law, lay no burden
Upon the backs of your poor fellowmen!

You, Pharisees, be not like sepulchers-
Clean outside, inside filled with filthy odours!
Wash not only the inside of cups and saucers,
And, you publicans, be not like ravenous vultures!"

The Lord's way have I come to prepare
Before His coming, the ground to lay bare.
His shoe lace to untie I'm not worthy -
So mighty and holy is He!"

"I've been sent to baptize you in water,
But, He will baptize you with Holy Ghost fire!
Let every heart be made clean
So your good works may be seen!"

7.

TO THE FATHER

Who, Father, can fathom the height of Your
Greatness?
Before the world was made, You reigned in Holiness!
You spoke this universe into full existence!
At Your Word, there appeared the Earth and the
Heavens!
The sun You created by day to give its light;
The moon Your Hand moulded to give its light by
night!
The stars Your Hand fashioned the night sky to adorn
—
But one, the Morning Star, You kept aside until Your
Son was born!
When man You created,
Your work was completed,
Polished and perfected.
In Your very likeness,
He, the Morning Star, walked in holiness
And perfect sinlessness!

8.
TO THE HOLY SPIRIT

O Thou, Spirit of Grace and Truth,
With Thy voice clear and smooth,
My soul Thou quieteth,
My mind Thou quickeneth
For Thou art God the Almighty
Reigning in all eternity!
O Thou, sweet Spirit of power,
Since the earliest hour
On Eternity's clock,
Thou hast been taking stock
Of what was to be created
And therein participated!
O Thou, Spirit, Thou art the Dove
Who, to show Thy great love,
On His Head came to rest
The Christ to manifest,
As in the cool Jordan He stood
Before the sinful multitude!
O Holy Spirit of Wisdom,
The way to God's Kingdom
Thou to Man showest
As on the Word he rests.
Indeed, Thou alone hast the art
Of convicting the human heart!
O Thou, my Holy Comforter,
Sent by Christ, my Saviour,

Poured out on Pentecost
To call sinner and lost!
Thy precious gifts to have I yearn,
Thy many fruits to bear I burn!

9.

TO MY BELOVED ONES

I, the Lamb, My life have come to give
So that whosoever will believe
In Heaven one day shall live
And the Crown of Life receive!

My glory in Heaven
Have I forsaken
My people to relieve of their burden
And their chains and fetters to see broken.

Satan, the father of lies,
Proved too strong a match for Adam unwise.
The Garden filled with bitter cries —
For die he must, who My Father's Word defies!

Fleeing from My Father's Face,
He walked away in utter disgrace
And all the human race
His lot must now embrace.

But down My life I lay
The price of salvation to pay
For I'm the Truth, the Life, the Way,
For those who to My Father pray.

10.

THE OTHER SERMON ON THE MOUNT
(Matthew 5 – 7)

Seek thee first my Kingdom,
Pray that it will soon come.
Thy neighbour help and love
One day to live above.
The poor do not reject,
But feed, love and respect.
Abhor idolatry,
Adore the Trinity.
Thy neighbour do not judge.
To thy enemies bear no grudge.
Father, mother honour;
Brother, sister succour.
Children do not despise,
To none speak ye lies.
Do not bear false witness,
Thy transgressions confess.
Condemn adultery,
Reject hypocrisy.
Ask and thou shalt receive,
Give and thou shalt relieve!
Seek and thou shalt find,
When offended, don't mind.
Knock and they shall open,
Show love to every man.

When struck on either cheek,
Keep cool and calm and meek.
When asked to give thy coat,
Do also give thy cloak.
When asked to go one mile,
Go two if thou aren't senile!
Pester not thy neighbor,
For thy own bread, labour!
These precepts if practised,
Thy reward thou won't miss.
If thou listenest to me,
My disciple thou shalt be.
If My commandments thou dost not despise,
These principles heed and practise.

11.

THE MIRACULOUS CATCH OF FISH

(Luke 5: 1 – 10)

There stood Jesus on the beach
The multitude to teach.
But so compact was the press —
Four thousand men, not less! —
That His voice could not carry.
The clue did not tarry:
Sighting a boat in the bay,
To it made He His way.
Seated in the moored vessel,
Parables He did tell
Of the Kingdom of Heaven
He'd come to preach to Man.
When His sermon was over,
Jesus turned to Peter:
"Steer thy boat into the deep
A mighty catch to reap."
"Sir, all night long we've laboured
Without a fish favoured."
But upon Thy Word I'll act
And from faith not detract."
Into the deep Peter moved
For his faith to be proved.
He picked up his idle net,
And cast it into the wet.

When aboard the net was brought,
His friends' help Peter sought:
So teeming with fish was it,
It wouldn't long resist!
Fish of every type and size —
Unseen by human eyes!
Two boatloads of fish they took,
That the boats, themselves, shook!
Stunned, on his knees Peter fell
The Lord Jesus to tell:
"Get Thee hence from me, Master,
For I'm a poor sinner!"
"Nay," the Lord Jesus replied,
With Me thou must abide.
Men I'll send thee now to fish
To rid of sin's blemish."
Leaving behind kith and kin,
Peter went souls to win.
The moment he left that beach,
Peter set off to preach,
To teach and cast out demons,
Lay hands on sick persons,
And men call to repentance
Under the Lord's guidance.

12.

CONVERSATION AT JACOB'S WELL
(John 4: 7 – 42)

"Will ye, woman, give me water?
This well is such a cool shelter!
To buy some food I've sent Peter,
I'll take a drink but eat later."
"How come thou, Jew, speakest to me?
Samaritans you treat lowly!
People of this territory
You, Jews, do treat indignantly."
"Woman, the water from this well,
Thy profound thirst will never quell.
But if, woman, thou knewest me well,
Thou with me wouldst not dare quarrel.
Living water I've come to give
To those who thirst and will receive.
Eternally with me they'll live,
If only in me they believe."
This well, Jacob, our forefather,
Gave to us ere he passed over.
But give me, Master, of that water,
For I'm weary of coming hither!"
"I am willing to quench thy thirst.
But bring to me thy husband first!"
"Master, I'm a woman accursed —
Of all women, the very worst!"

"I know husbands thou hast not four —
But five or six or maybe more!
That's why people call thee a whore!
I've seen how much thy heart is sore.
Repent, woman, and thy tears pour.
Quit the life thou livest before,
And obey now My Father's Law.
Go, woman, go and sin no more.
Cheer up, daughter, smile and be brave.
The Son of Man has come to save
Every sinner — from whore to knave,
And raise them one day from the grave!"
And into the city she ran,
Calling every Samaritan
To come and see that foreign Man
Who all her sins had forgiven.
"Come, people, come. Come see a Man
Who my sin's revealed and forgiven!
Come, people, see — Hallelujah!
A Prophet — Nay, the Messiah!"

13.

THE RAISING OF LAZARUS
(John 11: 1 – 44)

When her poor brother, Lazarus,
Fell ill, Martha ran to Jesus.
Off she rushed in great despair,
The cool air blowing through her hair.

All along the way, she prayed thus:
"Please, Father, empower Jesus,
Thy Son, a miracle to work
To break the pangs of Death that lurk!"

Reaching the place where Jesus was,
A crowd she saw with hurts and scars.
And she watched, as the Master healed
And the demon possessed rolled and reeled!

Threading her way through the thick crowd,
She fell before Jesus and bowed.
"Master, Master, I beseech Thee,
Do come my brother Lazarus to set free!

With sickness he is bed-confined;
He's pined away for he's not dined.
Quick, Master, quick! Do come home, please,
Lazarus' suffering to ease!"

Seeing poor Martha's affliction,
The Lord was moved with compassion.
"Weep not, woman. Let thy faith rise
And wipe those tears from thy sore eyes.

I'll go and thy dear brother heal.
Anon he'll rise and take his meal."
So off they went to Martha's place,
Through the crowd hastening their pace.

But ailing people on the way,
For their healings, too, came to pray.
With compassionate love and care,
The Lord stopped, their health to repair.

But soon down the street came Mary:
"Oh, Martha, why didst thou tarry?
Worry the Master not," she wept,
Our dear brother is gone and left!"

Hearing this, Martha's faith just fell.
Her tears flowed like water from a well.
She cried: "Hadst Thou been there, Master,
I still would have my dear brother!"

With firm confidence, Jesus spoke:
"Come on, Martha, lay down thy yoke.
Pluck all thy faith and just believe,
And thy brother shall surely live!"

As they walked on to Martha's place,
The Master spoke words of solace:

"Only believe and you will see
Manifested the Lord's glory!"

Thus encouraged, the two sisters
Led Jesus to the sepulchres
In one of which lay Lazarus,
While all around arose a fuss.

Lifting his eyes up to the skies,
Amidst a din of yells and cries,
Jesus calmly prayed: "O, Father,
My prayers You always answer.

Grant a miracle here and now
So to Your Name this crowd will bow!"
The stone He asked to be removed
For God's power to be proved.

"Nay," objected the crowd, "he stinks!"
"I'll bring him back over the brinks!
The stone remove and stand aside!!"
Anon the tomb lay open wide.

Forth came the voice — firm and fiery:
"Come forth, Lazarus, here hurry!"
And, behold, out came the deceased,
From Death's merciless grip released!

As everybody gazed, bemused, —
Seeing a dead man walk, unused, —
Jesus ordered: "His grave garments,
Loosen, for gone are his torments!"

And Lazarus and his sisters
Hurried back home, singing praises —
For never would they have believed
Somebody dead again could live!

14.

THE WOMAN WITH THE ISSUE OF BLOOD
(Matthew 9: 20 -22; Luke 8: 43 – 48)

For twelve long years, she lay crippled in bed,
Unable to be adequately fed.
Pain she had much; peace of mind she had none.
Great was the damage her disease had done!
It was a terrible issue of blood
That continuously flowed like a flood.
Many a great physician had she seen,
But worse and worse the poor thing's state had been.
Nobody did she have to care for her —
Neither a son, nor servant, nor sister!
A useless human rag had she become,
Waiting daily in death to find freedom.
Nailed to her bed by that awful disease,
She had long hoped that fatal flow would cease.
Day by day closer to death she was drawn,
And, like Job, cursed the day when she was born.
However, on her couch lying prostrate,
She'd heard how the storm Jesus did abate,
How loaves and fishes He had multiplied
A large crowd to feed, that else would have died!
How all manners of sicknesses He healed
And unclean spirits to Him had to yield.
How lepers He cleansed and how the dead He
raised!

For such miracles, she gave God the praise.
One day, however, such news reached her ears
That made her at once wipe away her tears:
Jesus would be passing through her village!
Her faith surged like from a fountain with rage!
Weak as she was, she rose from that bloody bed
That her shameful disease had turned all red.
Almost crawling, she left, Jesus to meet.
Painfully, she reached the hot teeming street
O how the press around Jesus was dense!
How merciless the heat and how intense!
Her whole body ached, but firm she remained.
As she spied in the press Jesus' long train.
"If I can only touch the hem of His garment,
I know gone will be my sad predicament!"
Such were the words she kept on repeating
Like a prayer fervently reciting.
Through the thick crowd threaded she her hard way
—

The hem of Jesus' robe being her prey.
Many a time she was pushed; oft she fell.
But nothing could the fire of faith quell!
Eventually, the hem got within reach
Because Jesus had stopped the crowd to teach.
Holding out her hand, hard she held His hem.
The flow stopped dead thanks to her stratagem!
She felt refreshed and revigorated;
New life made her feel rejuvenated.
Knowing what had happened, Jesus turned round,
Saying with a firm voice: "Who touched My gown?"
The disciples found this question silly.

"How come," they said, "Thou asketh<*Who touched Me?*>?
Thou art pressed by the crowd on every side.
We're all touching Thee — that cannot be denied!"
"Nay," Jesus answered, "somebody did touch Me!
I felt the touch of Faith on My Body,
And out of My Self flowed healing virtue!"
Thus, Jesus the whole situation knew.
No longer could the woman hide away.
Falling down before Jesus, she did say:
"Forgive me, Lord, it was I who touched Thee
Because of that bloody curse that plagued me."
With compassion, Jesus told the poor soul:
"Fear not, woman, thy faith has made thee whole!"
Away went the woman weeping with joy,
Proud such faith she'd been able to deploy.

15.
THE HEALING OF A "DOG"
(Matthew 15: 22 – 28)

When she found that her daughter was demon-
possessed,
That Syro-Phenician woman was sore distressed.
Into fits and seizures the demon would throw her,
Making her roll and reel, scream and shout and
shudder.
The girl, enslaved by such a powerful legion,
Would oft do things without any rhyme or reason:
Her old mother, herself, she would grab and aggress;
Her neighbours — for no reason — mistreat and
molest.
Held hostage to such heinous hellish hosts, the girl
Would that sort of erratic behaviourunfurl.
Seeing the girl's pitiful plight, the poor mother
Knew the demons would sooner or later kill her.
How could she see her daughter in such a torment?
She decided she should act and not just lament!
She had, of course, heard of Jesus of Nazareth
Who could even snatch people from the hands of
Death!
His help for her daughter she envisaged to seek —
For she had heard Jesus was a man mild and meek.
Somehow something worried her: she was Canaanite
Whereas Jesus had come for the Israelite!

Eventually, she decided to do something.
After hesitating and dilly-dallying,
She cast aside shame and fear, and went to Jesus:
"Master, Master, mercy on us, mercy on us!"
The disciples, on seeing her, chased her away.
But, undaunted, the poor woman went on to say:
"Master Jesus, Master Jesus, from oppression
Of the devil, save, please, my precious possession!
A daughter have I at home, severely oppressed
By fiends - themselves by a killing instinct obsessed!
O, Master, do come and from bondage set her free,
For I've heard of the wonderful works wrought by
Thee!"
Turning round, Jesus said: "Woman, how can I give
To dogs food that My children alone must receive?"
The words were harsh and hard, but meant her faith
to test.
Unoffended, the woman chose to act modest.
"Master," she said, "You're right: to dogs the
children's bread
Must not be thrown for fear the children go unfed.
But don't dogs feed on crumbs from the children's
table?
Give but the crumbs and that would be formidable!"
What of faith and modesty a demonstration!
Jesus for the dame was full of admiration —
Especially as she was Gentile — a non-Jew,
A foreign race to which salvation was not due.
"O, woman, what a formidable faith thou hast!
Thy daughter's oppression will hence no longer last!

Go, for thy daughter has from the demons been freed."
Grateful, woman went away with words of praise, indeed.

16.
BARTIMAEUS' SIGHT RESTORED
(Mark 10: 46 – 52)

By a roadside in Jericho
Sat the blind man, Bartimaeus.
As past him city folks would go,
He would cry out amidst the fuss:

"Pray, a coin or some bread do give
A poor and blind beggar to feed
So his accursed body may live —
For death looms over him, indeed!"

In his lice-ridden rags sat he
Day after day feeding on food
His tearful eyes just could not see.
Often the crowd to him was rude.

One day, as he sat there begging,
Looking famished and despondent,
A massive press he heard
And wondered what, on earth, it meant.

"Will you, please, tell a poor beggar
What's going on in Jericho!
If food they're coming to offer,
I sure, good folks, would like to know!"

"Bartimaeus, Bartimaeus,
The multitude that thou dost hear
Accompanies the man Jesus —
People coming from far and near!"

"Jesus, Jesus, Son of David!"
He cried. "Do have mercy on me!"
The crowd, not liking what he did,
Yelled: "Peace, thou knave, or we'll beat thee!"

But louder still the beggar cried:
"Jesus, on me do have mercy —
A poor beggar by the roadside
With eyes that stare but cannot see!"

Soaring above the din, his cries
Reached Jesus' compassionate ears
And He, before everyone's eyes,
Stopped with eyes welling with tears.
"Bring," He ordered, "this man to me!"
And, daunted, they told the beggar:
"Be of good cheer for He calls thee."
And they led him to the Master.

Now Bartimaeus had a coat
That he used to keep himself warm —
A ragged coat smelling of goat
That he threw, Jesus' purity not to harm.

"What wilt thou have me do for thee,
Thou wretched man?" questioned Jesus.
"O, good Master, that I may see!"

Implored at once Bartimaeus.

"Go, for thy faith hast made thee whole."
Promptly the beggar's sight was restored
And peace invaded his soul
Thanks to Jesus, his new-found Lord.

17.
ZACCHAEUS FORGIVEN AND SAVED
(Luke 19: 1 – 10)

A man there was called Zacchaeus —
A vile sinner like most of us.
A publican in Jericho,
No doubt, he had many a foe.
Collecting taxes, he cheated,
Poor folks' money he exacted.
Bound by a passion for money,
On the highway to Hell was he!
Soon his ill-gotten wealth would prove
Impossible with him to move.
For, in the after-world, riches
Are futile, the Lord's Word teaches.
One day, news came to Zacchaeus:
Jericho would receive Jesus!
He realized that was his chance
Of a lifetime to do penance,
To make amends for his mischief
And no longer be a thief.
As this man was of small stature,
Anon he tried hard to figure
How to catch a glimpse of Jesus
Amidst a crowd so numerous.
Up a sycomore-tree climbed he,
And there waited he patiently

The passage of the Lord to see.
Then a rumour rose, long and loud,
And he knew soon he'd see the crowd.
Indeed, the multitude arrived —
The lame, the blind and the deprived.
There, in the middle of the press,
Came Jesus in His long white dress.
Closer and closer the Christ drew
To present a full bird's eye view.
But in a great state of unrest
Was Zacchaeus up in his nest:
Should Jesus spy him in his tree,
He might expose his dishonesty!
One more step and Jesus would stand
Right below the tormented man.
Indeed, Jesus' gaze up the tree
Was attracted instinctively:
Zacchaeus was so tormented,
The poor fellow nearly fainted!
"Hurry down the tree, Zacchaeus!" —
When he heard himself addressed thus,
The crook grew even more anxious.
Meanwhile, all around them, no fuss
Could be heard: the din had died down,
Christ's voice being the only sound —
"For I must tonight sup with thee."
The rogue almost fell off the tree!
Imagine his astonishment
When he heard words so adamant!
Down the tree, hastily he got
To prepare a meal nice and hot.

But first fell he on bended knees,
Saying to Jesus: "Master, please,
The poor sinner I am, forgive.
A new life I want to live.
If my fellowmen I have robbed,
Restitution I make," he sobbed.
Lifting him up, Jesus declared,
As, stunned, the huge crowd stood and stared:
"Salvation has visited thee:
From sin, Zacchaeus, be set free!"
Relieved and grateful, Zacchaeus
Hurried home to feast with Jesus.
Those outside were green with envy,
Seeing the generosity
Shown to the sinful publican.
But Zacchaeus now forgiven,
No longer was he a sinner,
Thanks to Jesus, His Redeemer!

18.

THE PRODIGAL SON
(Luke 15: 11 – 32)

I

A man there was who was meek and wealthy.
In the country with his two sons lived he.
Vast acres of rich land did he possess
And his fat flocks nobody could assess.

II

On his vast lands grew corn and wheat and oats;
In his pastures grazed pigs and sheep and goats.
Scores of servants had he — male and female —:
The wealthiest man was he in the vale.

III

Two sons had he, who were his greatest pride.
Kind they were and would by his word abide.
These two sons were his sole and lucky heirs
And, in their father's wealth, had equal shares.

IV

Happily they managed their property,
Feasting, revelling and making merry

Amidst the sound of music and laughter.
Never was a family happier!

V

One day, however, the younger son said:
"Father, with thee long enough have I stayed.
Life in this dale is dull — destiny dark:
All day long, cows moo, sheep bleat, farm-dogs bark!

VI

Give me my share of the inheritance
So that I may quickly get away hence.
A better life I want to live in the city
Where the pleasures of youth are calling me."

VII

Deeply distressed was his dear old daddy.
Without his second son what would life be?
He knew of the city the temptations,
The numerous lures and the seductions.

VIII

To those, many a youth has been victim.
So his dad wisely tried to dissuade him.
But, when the spirit of adventure calls,
The wisest father's strongest objection falls!

IX

Accordingly, his wealth he divided
And his younger son did as had decided:
Kissing his brother and father goodbye,
Off to the city went the careless guy.

X

His father's house, in the young man's absence,
Settled into a sepulchral silence.
The sound of his voice no more cheered the house,
His laughter ceased his dad's joy to arouse.

XI

When the young man arrived in the city,
Hardly could he believe what he could see:
Clubs, ballrooms, restaurants and casinos;
Shops, bars, hotels, racing tracks and discos!

XII

The city lights flashed like a million stars,
The streets bustled with bikes, buses and cars.
"Why," he wondered, "did I not come before
Such pleasures to indulge in even more?"

XIII

Soon around him flocked friends and city folk:

Their ravenousness his rare wealth awoke.
To places went he where he shouldn't be,
Spending there his father's hard-earned money.

XIV

He paraded women of every sort
And did the most gorgeous city girls court.
Ah! How famous grew he — how sought after!
And blindly his money he did squander.

XV

The teetotal turned into a drunkard,
Tobacco to resist he found so hard.
With wealth-minded whores kept he company —
In short, he dived deep into debauchery!

XVI

It never rains but pours, the proverb says.
Soon on the horizon loomed gloomy days:
His blind inconsiderate lavishness
Left him broke and utterly penniless!

XVII

Friends forsook him; whores went with him no more.
Ah, what bitter tears he was led to pour!
His clothes were now all ragged and tattered
And from place to place, lonely, he wandered.

XVIII

His untrimmed hair grew long, his beard bushy.
There now emanated from his body
Not of costly perfume the rich fragrance,
But a foul and filthy smell of pestilence.

XIX

Famine having broken out in the land,
Starvation stared in the face our young man.
So, to keep body and soul together,
He became swineherd to a hard master.

XX

Even the swine's food he wanted to eat,
His unbearable hunger to defeat.
But no-one was there to give it to him.
Such was the high price he paid for his whim!

XXI

One day, as he sat watching the pigs eat,
In that far away land's sweltering heat,
Back home to his father his mind wandered,
And on his vain rebellion he pondered.

XXII

"What rich food I used to eat as a son —
Pork, beef, chicken, mutton and venison.
But now, as a stranger in this damned land,
Even on pig's food I cannot depend!

XXIII

My father's servants, themselves, eat their fill
And are allowed to drink as much they will.
But here I sit, forsaken and forlorn —
Famished! To feed on, not an ear of corn!

XXIV

But from this dung heap I will rise and pack,
And to my father's house promptly go back!
I'll tell him: "*Please, father, forgive your son
For having acted out of rebellion.*

XXV

*I have sinned against God and against thee,
As your child, do not now consider me.*"
Anon up he got and left everything.
Back home went he, along the way weeping.

XXVI

Ah, what a hard and bitter road he trod!
His blistered feet ached, for he went unshod.

Insects pestered him, stray dogs barked at him.
Never had somebody's life been so grim!

XXVII

In his absence, however, his dear dad
Grew so sad and sick, he almost ran mad.
He neither ate nor drank — sleep he knew not:
His whole life turned into a juggernaut.

XXVIII

Yet, down deep inside he had a firm trust:
Sooner or later, return his son must!
All day long, the horizon he observed,
Confident his son's life God had preserved.

XXIX

One morn he looked towards the horizon:
Afar he saw what looked like a person.
Gradually the figure closer grew.
His faith was ignited and, lo, he knew!

XXX

Oh yes, he knew his son it had to be!
Notwithstanding his age, he ran quickly
With arms wide open his son to receive,
And gave him the warmest hug he could give.

XXXI

The lad started to voice his confession,
But his voice broke with contrite emotion.
Unable to break their embrace, they wept,
The child with his tears repaying his debt.

XXXII

When the well of tears had dried up in him,
The old man's feature was no longer dim.
Petulant joy shone on his wrinkled face
And home he ordered his servants to race.

XXXIII

"Fetch for my son a new robe — clean and neat,
And a new pair of sandals for his feet.
Bring a gold ring as well for his finger
For my son today I want to honour!

XXXIV

Go and kill the fattened calf for a feast —
Such an event well deserves the best beast!
Let there be music, singing and dancing,
Let the vale resound with merry-making!

XXXV

For my son, who was lost, has now been found;
My son, who was dead, is now safe and sound!"

The servants rushed, the son's feast to prepare,
While, contrite, he bathed in fatherly care.

XXXVI

While the celebration was going on,
There returned from the fields the elder son.
When the singing and the dancing he heard,
A servant he summoned and enquired:

XXXVII

"What is all that commotion going on?
What's that music I hear from the mansion?"
"Thy brother is back," the servant answered,
"And thy father today wants him to be honoured."

XXXVIII

Instead of going in to make merry,
He grew indignant and became sulky.
A servant his old father had to call
To persuade him to come join in the ball.

XXXIX

"Father," he reproached, "I've always served thee
And never from thee exacted a fee.
Not a kid did I receive for my friends,
And, yet, never did I go away hence!

XL

That ungrateful son of thine thy money
Has spent with friends and whores in the city.
Thy work and thy presence he neglected
And left thee here sad and broken-hearted.

XLI

Now upon him thou bestowesthonour
And grantest this fiend fatherly favour...”
Oh, how the father was bitterly grieved,
Hearing how his elder son his junior received.

XLII

But the father loved them both equally.
So to the elder son spoke he calmly:
“My son, it is true thou hast been faithful
And thy presence always made me cheerful.

XLIII

Everything I own is thy property.
As for the kid, to kill thou hadst merely.
But thy brother was lost and is now found;
Was dead, as it were, and has now come round.

XLIV

His case is entirely different.
Do come in to celebrate this event!”

Ashamed of his unbrotherly conduct,
The son confessed it was a turn of luck.

XLV

"Forgive me, father, for my callous heart.
I swear with my brother I'll now act smart."
When they went in and brother hugged brother,
In the father's heart it was like summer!

XLVI

He wept all his tears out — warm tears of bliss:
His younger son rescued from the abyss!
All through the night, they rejoiced and revelled —
A son to celebrate, who once rebelled.

19.
THE TRANSFIGURATION
Matthew 17: 1 -9; Mark 9: 2 – 10)

Leaving the Nine behind,
Upon yonder mount Jesus climbed
With Peter, James and John
When all the multitude was gone.

Wrapped in the garb of solitude,
He prayed with fervent solicitude:
"May Thy glory shine, Father,
So these Three can testify later."

And, lo, His Face shone as bright as daylight
And His complexion turned immaculately white.
Breaking away from overpowering sleep,
The Three gazed in contemplation deep:

Behold, there stood Moses — all patient and meek —
,
And Elijah, the fiery prophet, on that mountain peak!
Then a Voice thundered from Heaven:
"This is My Beloved Son; to Him, hearken!"

Still in a daze, having beheld so sublime a wonder,
The Three followed, speechless, the Master,
The Nine others to tell

How on yonder mount, Heaven's glory fell!

57

20.

THE QUEEN OF SHEBA VISITS KING SOLOMON
so(1 Kings 10; 2 Chronicles 9; Matthew 12:42)

I
(PROLOGUE)

As soon as king David was declared dead,
Solomon came to the throne in his stead.
But what a heavy legacy
And what enormous responsibility
That fell upon that man
So young and tender then!

II

It was no easy thing
To be appointed king
Over a land so vast
With such a glorious past –
A people so numerous
And, quite often, rebellious!

III

One night, as the king lay
After a long and weary day,
The Lord, in a clear vision,

Brought him consolation
Because the king's father
Had always had the Lord's favour.

IV

"Come on, Solomon"
Came the Word of the Lord anon,
"Whatever thou most desirest
I'll see that thou acquirest –
Gold canst thou have in abundance,
Much silver I can to thee dispense".

V

"Ah, Lord God," replied the king,
"My kingship is already a wondrous thing.
To reign over Thy people is so awesome,
All I require of Thee is wisdom"
So that of David, my father,
I can be a worthy successor".

VI

So pleased was the Lord with that reply,
Solomon's request He couldn't deny.
"Silver and gold thou askest not,
A long life, if asked, thou couldst have got.
Thou couldst have wished thy enemies dead,
Wisdom askest thou instead…"

VII

"Therefore, wisdom I give to thee
No man like thee will there ever be.
Moreover, I'll give to thee riches untold –
Precious stones, silver and gold.
Thy fame and thy fortune will travel far
Kings and queens will come to thee from afar".

VIII

Indeed, Solomon's fame spread far and wide
Kings and queens found in him a guide.
In judgment he was formidable -
His verdicts were most laudable!
With abundant wealth, too, he was blessed –
Such as no man had ever witnessed!

IX

Solomon's fame reached distant Ethiopia
Where reignedMalikat, Queen of Sheba.
As she was wise and wealthy, too,
She believed not what she was told was true.
One day, therefore, she made up her mind
To journey to Israel herself to find.

X

With precious stones, sandal wood, silver and gold

In caravans she went to verify what she'd been told.
For days and days, did she travel
To confer with Solomon in distant Israel,
Devising ways to do her best
Solomon's exceptional wisdom to test.

XI

Once introduced into the king's presence,
Queen Malikat was struck by the unparalleled
magnificence:
Never before had she witnessed such glamour
Nor set her eyes upon such splendour -
The palace, the dishes, the food, the cutlery -
Even the king's servants' livery!

XII

Now came the time for interrogation.
Malikat asked question after question:
Questions on ethics, on politics, on diplomacy, on
administration …
But Solomon demonstrated impeccable erudition!
Flabbergasted, the Queen of the South
Relished every word pouring out of Solomon's mouth!

XIII

Deeply impressed by all she had heard and seen
Queen Malikat now had her conscience clean.
She ordered that all the treasures she'd brought
Be taken to the king's Court.
Sandal wood, precious stones, gold and silver

Were brought Solomon to honour.

XIV

The king, in return, upon Queen Malikat showered
Even more presents than he had been offered.
The Queen asked of the king whatever she wanted
And every one of her demands was granted.
More than satisfied with all she had seen, heard and received,
Malikat to Sheba returned, her conscience amply relieved.

XV

(EPILOGUE)

Jesus warns us that, on Judgment Day,
The Queen of the South will come and say:
*"Why did you not listen to the One God sent
To impress upon you the need to repent?
I to Israel went the wise Solomon to see,
But infinitely greater than Solomon is He!"*

21
THE RICH MAN AND LAZARUS
(Luke 16: 19 – 31)

I

There once was a man wealthy and opulent.
Purple and fine linen constituted his princely garment.
Daily feasted he on choice meat and costly wine.
All day long, like a glutton, did he dine.
Crystal chandeliers hung from the ceiling –
Brightening up every nook of the building.

II

At his door, sat one Lazarus, a poor beggar -
Ugly and unsightly sores did his body cover.
His sores, dogs from the street came to lick,
As he lay agonising on the threshold brick.
And longing for crumbs from the rich man's table.
But heartless was he - so selfish and detestable!

III

All day long, Lazarus sent prayers to heaven.
Thereby hoping his sufferings to lessen.
Down deep inside, somehow, he knew
Somewhere there was a world so pure and new.
The world of that wealthy man, instead,

Was made up only of meat, wine and bread.

IV

Death, however, was just around the corner
Inexorably lying in ambush for the one as for the
other.
With what relief Lazarus breathed his last:
With what joy his misery and sufferings did he cast!
But, lo, an angelic host saw he,
Ushering him into a world of glee!

V

But the once rich man landed into a lake of fire
Never had he suspected there was a place so dire!
All around him did gigantic flames leap
And wriggling worms all over him did creep!
A strange fire it was that burned but died not!
Nowhere on earth had he heard of a place so hot!

VI

Looking up, Lazarus did he see in sweet repose
And wondered what of his state could be the cause.
Then he saw old Abraham in Lazarus' company:
"Father Abraham," cried he, "have mercy!"
"Do send Lazarus my dried tongue with water to
cool!"
"Forgive me, on earth, for having been such a fool!"

VII

"I'm sorry, my child," came Abraham's reply,
"No matter how loudly you may cry,
"Lazarus can, in no way, cross over to you
The chasm between us is far wider than you ever
knew!"
Neither can you come join us here
For we are worlds apart, though we look so near!"

VIII

"Please, Father Abraham, I have five brothers selfish
as I,
They, too, will end up here in this fire as time goes by:
Do send Lazarus to them with a word of warning!"
"It's enough to Moses and the prophets they started
listening."
"No, Father Abraham, Moses and the prophets they
despise.
But caution given by one from the Dead can make
them wise!

IX

"No, my child, if Moses and the prophets your
brothers scorn,
They won't listen, even if a dead man be reborn!
You see, Lazarus, on earth, spent a life of misery and
agony

Never once a piece of bread threw you to him out of mercy.
His hunger is now forever appeased and his sores forever healed
But for your selfish living on earth, your fate is now eternally sealed!"

22

THE BARGAIN

(Matthew 26; Mark 14; Luke 22; John 18)

Most Reverend High Priest,
I come to offer you
A deal you can't resist:
The most notorious Jew —
Jesus of Nazareth!
A prey so hard to find —
A man to put to death!
But what worries my mind:
How much are you prepared
To pay for such a prey?
For my repute impaired,
You know, Reverend High Priest,
My costs I must defray —
Forty pieces of silver at least.
Too high a price, you say?
Twenty pieces cash down?
Thirty pieces, O.K.
I'll see you get the clown!
The place: Gethsemane.
The cue: the Judas' kiss.
O Sir, quick get the money,
This deal you sure can't miss!

23
GETHSEMANE
(Matthew 26; Mark 14)

Gethsemane, Gethsemane!
Garden of woe
Ground of sorrow
Get thee ready, Get the money.

Canst thou not hear their footsteps near?
The Iscariot
His price he's got!
With clubs and spears they're coming here!

Wake Peter up, I see the Cup.
Father, Father,
Move it farther.
Thy will be done — I've come to sup!

My life I give so they shall live.
I'm sweating blood —
Eternal bud!
Be not bereaved, My Blood receive!

Silent don't keep, Gethsemane.
See the torches —
It's My tortures!
Lament and weep, Gethsemane!

24

PONTIUS PILATE'S PROSECUTORY PROBLEM
(Matthew 27; Mark 15; Luke 23; John 18)

I

How I wish they hadn't sent Him to me here!
Couldn't Herod, himself, the case hear?
As king, full jurisdiction has he
Over the whole of Judea and Galilee!
And what about the priests
Annas and Caiaphas, to judge they aren't the least!

II

Already the mob has flocked outside
And their fury they wouldn't hide!
To know the verdict, they are all eager
And no dismissal they'd accept either!
How to deal with this, I do not know!
Hear how their howlings up to the Praetorium echo!

III

A note from my dear wife have I received
Lying on her couch, she doesn't feel relieved.
*"Make sure this Just you do not touch,
Drop the charges, leave Him as such!"*
How I wish I never was appointed by Rome

And lived a peaceful life at home!

IV

This Man have I meticulously examined
And not an iota of guilt in Him have I seen!
The Emperor exacts a guilty verdict
And who can this potentate contradict?
I know if I declare this Man guilty,
With myself, I'll never be at peace assuredly!

V

To make matters worse, the Passover is drawing nigh
And the people's demands are growing high.
As every year, they'll want a prisoner set free!
To this Just, I think I'll grant mercy.
From my balcony, I'll anon inform them,
However, I fear this triggers further mayhem!

VI

(*From his balcony, Pilate addresses the crowd*).

"People of Jerusalem, Judea and Galilee
For a moment, please, do hearken to me:
The Man Jesus have I fully examined
And not a single fault in Him have I determined!
To detain Him, therefore, I see no reason
As governor, I, Pontius Pilate, will release Him anon!"

VII

(*The crowd shouts to Pilate*)

"Crucify Him! Crucify Him! To death, the blasphemer!
An impostor – nay a Sabbath breaker!
Our Temple, He claimed to destroy and rebuild,
Only for that, deserves He to be killed!
With God even made He, himself, equal:
Scourge Him and crucify Him withal!"

VIII

(*Pilate addresses the crowd*)

"Whom, therefore, shall I release: Barabbas or
Jesus?"
"*Crucify the blasphemer, and Barabbas give back
unto us!*"
"See, therefore, in water do I wash my hand:
To meddle with this Man's blood I don't intend.
A Just, I know, shall I be condemning, alas!
Here hand I over to you a criminal – Barabbas!"
(*03 August 2021*).

25

SEVEN PRONOUNCEMENTS FROM THE CROSS
(Luke 23:34; Matthew 27:43; John 19: 26-27; Matthew 27:46; John 19:28; John 19: 30; Luke 23:46)

I

Here am I, Father, hanging on that Cross
Because of human injustice so gross.
Yet, men's souls came I to save
Their bodies to rescue from the grave.
Thirty pieces of silver for me they laid down
My brow they've adorned with a thorny crown!

II

And yet, from place to place went I
The devil and demons for them to defy.
All of their sicknesses did I heal
Dark secrets in their hearts did I reveal.
But here I am – to the wood nailed
Because man's justice lamentably failed!

III

Instead of me, they chose Barabbas

Such a criminal set they free, alas!
But I, the Son of man, have they crucified,
Spat upon, buffeted, mocked and vilified!
My beard they pulled most disrespectfully
My blood they caused to flow abundantly.

IV

Canst Thou hear, Father, their shouts around me
rising
Like bulls of Bashan brutishly bellowing?
"Crucify him ! Crucify him!" they yell.
Up, on Golgotha hill, I hear them well.
"Hail, thee, king of the Jews!" shout they in derision.
But let it be, Father, if it's their mad volition.

V

Oh, how the thorns in my crown they hurt!
The blood from my brow cause they to spurt.
The nails in my hands and feet my movements
restrain
From moving to left or right must I refrain.
And see, Father, this gaping hole in my side
That soldier's spear has made deep and wide!

VI

But forgive them, Father, their ignorance
For they know not of their actions the sense!
If only they knew whom they were crucifying,

They'd think wisely before acting.
Because the One they've crucified
Will one day soon their eternal fate decide!

VII

Here I hang, in two murderers' company.
The one on my left shamelessly curses me
The one on my right asks me to forgive.
"Tonight with me, in Paradise, thou shalt live!"
If only the other had been wise,
In Paradise, he, too, could live likewise!

VIII

But behold, who's there but Mary in the crowd
Lamenting amidst those shouts fierce and loud!
And there stands John, the beloved, too,
Sobbing as loudly as he can do!
"Woman, cry not for here is thy son!"
"And thee, John, here's thy mother from now on!"

IX

Now here I agonize, all forlorn,
My flesh all battered and torn.
All those I healed, taught and fed
In fear of death, have left and fled!
Eli, Eli, Lama Sabachthani,
Why hast thou forsaken me?

X

Not a single drop of blood is left in my veins,
Water from my side gushed like summer rains.
Oh! how for water *I thirst*, Father!
But all that my torturers give is vinegar!
Yet Living Water did I come to give
So those willing can drink and live!

XI

I can see now the end of this mockery -
The most glaring miscarriage of justice in history.
Hanna, Caïaphas, Herod, Pontius Pilate
Have all plotted to seal my fate!
My body flogged, my blood poured out, my faculties
diminished –
All I can say, Father, is: It is finished!

XII

See darkness now coming down
This whole sinful world to drown.
The Cup's been drunk to the lees
So men's miseries and oppression can cease.
Their souls have I rescued out of the pit.
Now, Father, into Thy hand my spirit do I remit.

(August 02, 2021)

26
WORDS FROM THE CROSS

Here on the Cross I hang
As Death, the hydra, projects its ugly fang.
In a while hence, it will all be finished:
I, the Son of God, to this shameful state diminished!

Never would it have crossed my mind
That Man, whom My Father created so kind —
In His very image, even — could deign
Such a state of inhumanity attain!

They hit Me, they flogged Me.
In royal garb they clothed Me out of mockery.
They buffeted Me, they spat on My face,
Putting the seal of excellence upon My disgrace.

The thorns in the crown, My brow they hurt,
The nails in My hands and feet, My Blood they cause
to spurt,
The spear wound in My side, my very entrails expose.
O come, Death, my soul yearns for repose.

Eli, Eli, Lama Sabatchtani!
I thirst, but vinegar is all they give to Me!
Darkness envelopes me now like an unfathomable
pit.
Father, unto Thy Hands, my spirit do I remit!

27
THE RESURRECTION
(Matthew 28; Luke 24)

On that bright Sunday morn,
The womenfolk all forlorn
To the cold Tomb they go
As tears down their cheeks flow.

Their Master's Death they mourn,
Who Man to save was born.
In solemn silence wrapped,
Their ointment jars they clasp.

In anguish, they wonder
How the Tomb to enter —
For the entrance is blocked
With an enormous rock!

At the Tomb sad and cold,
Behold, the rock's been rolled!
And, lo, an Angel they behold
And glad tidings they're told:

"Why, women, weep you thus?
He's risen, your Jesus!
Quick, run to the city
Go tell everybody!"

And off the women they go,
The glad tidings to sow,
As shouts of "He's risen!"
Fill the neighbouring glen.

28
THE ASCENSION
(Acts 1: 3 - 12)

Full forty days after Jesus's Resurrection,
The disciples, assembled together, saw an Apparition.
"Who can that be?" they wondered -
The Master's promise, they no longer remembered!
Soon the Apparition much clearer grew
And closer the benumbed disciples drew.
Then Jesus, the Risen Christ, did they recognize
Although appeared He in superhuman guise!

"Do ye, my beloved, not remember
I promised I'd send ye the Comforter –
Who in ye will forever abide
Into all truth to be to ye a guide?
John the Baptist baptized ye in water,
But the Holy Ghost, when He comes, will baptize ye
with fire!
From Jerusalem, therefore, depart ye not
Until Whom I've promised you've got.
Not many days hence, power will ye receive
That the Holy Ghost will give.
To all of Judea, to Samaria, to all of Galilee
And to the uttermost part of the world my witnesses
ye'll be!"

No sooner had He finished speaking,
Than, lo, the disciples to heaven saw Him rising!
As, to heaven looked they in utter amazement:
Behold, two Angels did appear in white raiment.
"Men of Galilee, why, stunned, watch ye this Jesus to heaven rise?
One day, He'll come back in exactly the same guise!"
Pondering those strange words by Angels uttered to them,
Down Mount Olivet did the disciples walk back to Jerusalem.

(03 August 2021)

29

UPON JESUS' ASCENDING TO HEAVEN

I

Welcome back home, my dear beloved Son.
Thou hast accomplished Thy noble mission
In a very impeccable manner.
On the Throne sit anew by Thy Father.

II

My perfect will, my Son, Thou hast performed,
Man's sinful nature to fully reform.
For Me, the past thirty-three years or so
Have been the hardest, as far as I know.

III

Oh, to be thus separated from Thee —
The only time in all Eternity!
But to this, Thou consented Man to save.
Be commended now for this act so brave!

IV

This to achieve, what a price Thou didst pay!
Back to Me to show Man the only way,
Here with Me Thou hadst to leave Thy glory

And put on the garb of humanity!

V

O what a magnanimous abasement!
Between Thee and Me, what an agreement!
Such love, Son, Man will never comprehend,
Such mystery he'll never understand.

VI

Thou took birth in a Bethlehem manger
With filth and animals helter skelter.
Thy torment started off very early:
Herod's sword into Egypt made Thee flee.

VII

When there started Thy public ministry,
Greater grew general hostility.
Thou facest unbelieving Sadducees
And, worse, hypocritical Pharisees!

VIII

Teachers of the Law called Thee blasphemer,
The Scribes were more ferocious than ever.
In Samaria, they would not have Thee,
To enter the Temple, they made Thee pay a fee!

IX

Satan, too, of Thee tried to make a fool.
But his vile tricks did himself ridicule.
O how My Word proved a mighty weapon
When, tempted, Thou just quoted It anon!

X

How naïve of him to think Thou wouldst bow
And adore him! ... Angels adore Thee now!
The storm on the lake, he made it happen.
Ah, how he thought he'd drown Thee there and then!

XI

This trick he played because the Gadarene,
Thou wouldst set free of the legion, he'd seen,
And Thy plan tried he to spoil — but in vain,
For by Thee all his hordes were utterly slain!

XII

How treacherous of him when, through Peter,
Thy way to the Cross he tried to hinder!
How I marvelled when Thou didst find him out:
"Get thee hence, Satan!" came Thy mighty shout.

XIII

Even on the Cross, he relentlessly
Harassed Thee to try to thwart Calvary!

"Come down," said he, "if Thou art the Saviour!"
But Thou held firm to be Man's Redeemer.

XIV

One man Thou called to be an Apostle
Proved to be of a very base mettle.
Indeed, Judas plotted and betrayed Thee,
Blinded by Mammon, the god of money.

XV

Thirty pieces of silver — that's the prize
He was offered for such a Holy Merchandise!
The field that he bought with that cursed money
His own burial ground turned out to be!

XVI

After Thy arrest, what a show they made:
Before Caiaphas they made Thee parade,
Before Hanna, his father-in-law, Thou wert dragged,
False witnesses brought they, that came and
bragged!

XVII

Before Herod Thou wast made to appear,
Who some wonder wanted to see or hear.
But his vile ambition Thou frustrated:
Miracles should not be lightly sported!

XVIII

Before Pontius Pilate, the governor,
Thou wast brought Thy accusers to answer.
In his own words, no wrong was found in Thee;
Yet he would not set Thee at liberty!

XIX

I solicited his wife in her sleep
So Pilate Thy integrity would keep.
But madly with the trial he went on.
How? ... Asking for the mob's verdict thereon!

XX

Ah, how that bloodthirsty multitude yelled!
How that ungrateful motley crowd rebelled!
They forgot their sicknesses Thou hadst healed,
The key to My Kingdom Thou hadst to them revealed!

XXI

When questioned, they wanted Thee crucified —
Barabbas out of jail and sanctified!
Never was there such an absurd trial —
Sheer mockery! And most illogical!

XXII

But, My Son, how could it have been otherwise?
Calvary had to be materialised!

An innocent death Thou sure hadst to die
Guilty humanity to sanctify!

XXIII

Remember, Son, the Plan of Salvation
We schemed when Adam fell to temptation?
That's just to what Thou and I consented:
Innocence condemned and guilt innocented!

XXIV

O, Son, the beauty of such a Plan!
How unique, Son! Just for the love of Man!
Just the Three of us to execute it:
I — YAHWE — Thee and the Holy Spirit!

XXV

Although in Thee no guilt Pilate had found,
The voice of his conscience he just turned down.
Asking them for water, he washed his hand
Before the crowd to show his innocence.

XXVI

Setting notorious Barabbas free,
He then to Thy torturers handed Thee.
Like rapacious vultures upon their prey,
The mob just grabbed Thee and dragged Thee away.

XXVII

The Roman soldiers that day had a feast:
Their pronged flog rose and hit Thee like a beast!
Thy back the cruel flog lacerated
As precious drops of Divine Blood were shed.

XXVIII

They mockingly dressed Thee in purple gown
And for Thy head plaited with thorns a crown.
And when Thy brow with the sharp thorns was
bruised,
Ah, what a fountain of Holy Blood oozed!

XXIX

Long Roman nails drove they into Thy feet
That went from place to place their needs to meet.
They hammered nails into Thy Holy Hands
That touched their sick bodies to heal and cleanse.

XXX

And when Thy Cross they raised on Calvary,
What a jubilation! What revelry!
The bloodthirsty hounds had come for their feast
Like bulls of Bashan tearing down a beast!

XXXI

Oh, Son, how they barked and brayed and bellowed!
And yet Thou camest to carry their load!
Also to feed them on the mountainside,
Thou hadst loaves and fishes multiplied!

XXXII

Even for Thy tunic soldiers cast dice:
To deprive Thee, what devilish device!
As on the Cross Thou wert agonizing,
A soldier at Thy side his spear did fling!

XXXIII

Through Thy wound how Thy Blood kept coming out!
Every single drop of it oozed, no doubt,
For, after Thou hadst bled, out came water
That flowed awhile, then nothing thereafter!

XXXIV

What magnanimity in Thy prayer:
"Forgive them for they do not know, Father,
What they are doing." How noble of Thee!
Thy Cross is where love met hostility!

XXXV

When, on the Cross, Thy battered Body hung

And, thirsting, to Thy palate Thy tongue clung,
All they gave Thee to drink was vinegar —
Yet, Thou gavest them Living Water!

XXXVI

Eli Eli Lama Sabatchtani!
Dost Thou know, my Son, why I forsook Thee?
Well, how could I, in all My Holiness,
Fix My eyes on all the world's wickedness?

XXXVII

For, on the Cross, Son, Thou becamest Sin
So sinners' souls Thy Sacrifice could win.
Thou becamest curse to eradicate
The curse that changed the whole of Man's fate.

XXXVIII

And, when Thy last breath Thou gavest,
What nobility Thou didst manifest!
"It is finished!" didst I hear Thee say.
Never has there been such a day!

XXXIX

Then the Heavenly Hero's final act
Thou, Son, didst magnanimously enact:
"Unto Thy Hands, Father, My Spirit do I remit."
O for an apotheosis, how fit!

XL

And, lo, all upon the Earth darkness fell —
Though it was broad daylight! — the world to tell
How solemn and dramatic a moment
It was when the Light of the World just went!

XLI

Indeed, Thy Spirit didst Thy Body leave,
Leaving Thy loved ones to mourn and grieve.
What an homage from the centurion:
"Behold, of God, indeed, was He the Son!"

XLII

From the Cross was Thy Body brought down,
Laid in a tomb in a burial ground.
The women went home, weeping and wailing.
"Why such wickedness?" they kept wondering.

XLIII

Three days and nights in the tomb didst Thou stay
For every sin ever made by Man to pay.
Dead in Body, but in Spirit active,
Thou kept labouring so dead souls could live!

XLIV

I laughed when I saw on the third morning
Women to Thy tomb gravely proceeding

With ointment pots Thy Body to embalm
In the early morning sunny and warm.

XLV

Weeping, they wondered who the stone would roll,
Unaware of what was soon to befall.
Imagine, at the tomb, their anxiety
When they saw it stood open and empty!

XLVI

"Why, women, do ye seek among the dead
He who from the dead is resurrected?"
At the Angel's bidding, away they ran,
Shouting: "He is risen! He is risen!"

XLVII

Ah, my dear Son, what a vindication
Over death through Thy grand resurrection!
The law of sin and death hast Thou broken,
The gates of the Kingdom now stand open!

XLVIII

Principalities have now been conquered,
Powers of darkness to Thee surrendered!
Chains, shackles and fetters hast Thou broken,
People's yokes and burdens hast Thou lightened!

XLIX

The ransom for captive Man hast Thou paid,
For, on the altar, Thy Life Thou hast laid.
To celebrate so great a victory,
I now bestow upon Thee My Glory!

L

I now give Thee above all names the Name
That will put Satan and his hordes to shame —
The one Name to which every knee shall bow
And every tongue confess Thou art Lord now.

LI

Be Thou made Lord of lords upon all things
And upon all flesh! Hail Thou, King of kings!
Thy Body have I glorified, O Son,
Never again to be pierced by weapon!

LII

Gone now is the crown so cruel and thorny:
Don hence the Eternal Crown of Glory!
Come sit at My right Hand while Thy enemies
I place under Thy feet and on their knees!

LIII

Angels will I command now to adore Thee
Day and night giving Thee praise and glory.

Their crowns at Thy Feet will they cast, singing:
"Praises, honour and glory to the King!

LIV

Angels and Archangels at Thy command
Will hasten to grant Thy every demand.
Cherubims and Seraphims shall surely
Minister to Thee, Son, diligently.

LV

For Thy mission Thou hast accomplished,
The law of sin and death, too, abolished.
A lost and doomed humanity rescued,
All the powers of Hell and Death subdued!

LVI

From Thy accomplished labour, come and rest,
For Thou hast shown Divine love at its best.
Let us be — the Holy Ghost, Thee and I —
Bonded anew by an eternal tie!

30

A CALL TO REPENTANCE

Thou who walkest in arrogance,
Who buildest around thee a fence,
As though none with thee can compare —
Thinking thou art a race so rare;
Thou who seekest self-justice,
Claiming thou never doest amiss,
Calling thyself just and upright
And to everybody a light;
Thou who walkest in pitch darkness,
In misery and loneliness,
Crossing the hot desert of life,
Struggling to still life's storms and strife;
Thou whose quick hands with blood are stained —
To thy past a captive enchained —
Who, of guilt, bearest deep the scars
Behind invisible jail bars;
O thou inveterate drinker,
Who never once is found sober,
Whose life spent in a tavern nook,
Whose wife, children and babe forsook;
And thou, poor heartbroken lover,
Whose heart didst lovingly offer
Only to be pierced by a dame
Too vain to wear thy accursed name,
Come all to that old rugged Cross

And all your sins and burdens toss
For Jesus Christ, your Redeemer,
Once died, but now lives forever!
His Blood He shed on Calvary
To snatch from the Adversary
Every one of you, poor sinners,
Destined to perish in hell's fires!
Every sin of yours He forgives,
Every one of you He receives
In Heaven's Eternal Abode.
But quit kicking against the goad!
Bid farewell to all your sorrows;
Come and find peace and sweet repose
In His loving arms wide open,
Ready to embrace every man.
Come and drink at Love's true fountain
And you'll never thirst again!
Come and feed freely on His Word.
Come quick all who this call have heard!

31
COME UNTO ME

Come unto me,
All you who thirst:
From Calvary
Fresh water bursts!
From my pierced Hands,
Life's Water flows!
So do come, friends,
And you, too, foes!

Come unto me,
You who hunger:
Without money,
Food I offer!
On my Word, feed,
And live for good
For Life, indeed,
Rests in my food!

Come unto me
You who labour;
From toil be free:
Rest I offer!
Lay down your yoke:
Come be my Bride.
Your yoke I broke,
Your tears I cried!

Come unto me,
All you who stray:
Without a fee,
In my Light, stay —
For I'm the Light
Come from Heaven
To give you sight
And Life, even!

32

JESUSCHRIST

(An Alexandrine Acrostic)

Just listen to my Word: the key is to believe -
Eternal life through me, if you believe, receive!
Salvation I purchased for you on Calvary.
Until I come to you, stand firm in faith and pray
So in Heaven you'll live: I am the only Way!

Calvary was the place where I, in agony,
Have shed my holy blood to save everybody.
Rising as I had said from the tomb where I lay,
Iwon a victory on Death with great display!
So fear no more, my child: I'm on my way to thee
To lift thee up with me where there's eternal glee!

33
PSALM OF REPENTANCE

O Lord of grace and mercy,
Humbly come I to Thee
To ask for Thy hand to be lifted off me
For Thy face to turn back to me
For against Thee I have sinned, Lord
Thy laws I have transgressed.

My sin, O Lord, I won't hide before Thee
Nor can I, O Lord, my iniquity conceal.
For Thou knowest everything
And Thy eye seest everything
Thou art the all-knowing God.
All of man's secrets are to Thee an open book.

Lord, here and now I cast before Thee
Each and every one of my sins.
Exercise Thy mercy, O Lord,
Against the helpless sinner I am
And all the days of my miserable life
I will serve Thee and be to Thee a child.

34
PSALM OF PROTECTION

O Lord, I come to Thee for help
For I am a man pursued and hunted.
My enemies are after me.
They have encompassed me,
Turning me into a prey.
What they want from me
Is the precious – invaluable gift
Thou hast bestowed upon me –
A gift so rare and so precious
Given to me to bring glory to Thy Name.
O Lord, please, don't let them snatch it from me
Don't let them rob me of it.
For it's a gift that cost me nothing,
But that cost Thee everything!
Send Thy holy angels, Lord,
In fiery chariots and with deadly darts
To chase them and make them flee.
Lord, hide me under Thy wings
Shelter me in the warmth of Thy bosom
For, only in Thy company am I secure.

35
PSALM OF PRAISE
(O LORD OF HOSTS)

O LORD of Hosts
Who is like unto Thee?
Thou art seated in high places
Holy Angels bow before Thee
And cast their crowns at Thy feet
As they sing Hallelujahs to Thee.
The sun, the moon, the stars
Are the workmanship of Thy hand
At Thy word, clouds gather
And cause rain to fall
The sun, at Thy will, shines in the firmament.

O LORD of Hosts,
Who is like unto Thee?
Thou with plagues broke Pharaoh's pride
To force him to set Thy people free
The waters of the Red Sea Thou causest to part
Pharaoh, his army, his soldiers, their horses and their
chariots
Thou caused to be engulfed in the waters
While Thy people Thou caused to cross dry-footed.
Manna Thou sent from heaven to feed Thy rebellious
people

Water Thou caused to gush out of a rock to quench
them
At Mara, Thou made bitter water sweet

O LORD of Hosts,
Who is like unto Thee?
The lofty impenetrable walls of Jericho
Was it not Thee who caused them to fall?
The Canaanites, the Philistines, the Ammorites and
the Moabites
Was it not Thee who brought them low
And their false gods cause to fall face down before
Thee?

O LORD of Hosts,
Who is like unto Thee?
O no, LORD, none is there like Thee
None so great, so holy, so majestic!
None so worthy of praise and glory
O LORD, Thou art God
Above every other god
And over all creation!

36
TO THE LAMB

O Lamb of God, born to be sacrificed,
A ransom to pay for man overpriced!
Thou wast given as God's free gift to Man
To show him the only way to Heaven.

Lamb of God promised the human race to redeem
Since Adam sinned and unworthy was deemed.
Thy young life, Thou camest to surrender,
Thy Holy Blood to shed on the altar!

Exalted now on high,
With Angels standing by,
Thy Name they glorify!

Their merry voices ring
As joyfully they sing:
"Hail to Thee, Jesus King!"

37
A PRAYER OF THANKSGIVING

Thank-You, Father, for Your Son
In Whom every believing person,
Can have, by confession and conviction:

Expiation,
Redemption,
Propitiation,
Justification,
Salvation,
Reconciliation
Adoption,
Sanctification
Resurrection,
Translation,
Glorification.

38

CONCLUSION

Dear reader,
You have now reached the end of this Anthology of Biblical Poems. I sincerely hope you have been blessed by those words inspired by God's Holy Spirit and that you have taken as much pleasure reading them as I have had writing them.

Those, I believe, were words well worth writing.

Dr Jean Norbert Augustin.

www.ingramcontent.com/pod-product-compliance
Lightning Source LLC
Chambersburg PA
CBHW071334140726
47996CB00005B/1976